DAD JOKES

The Good.
The Bad.
The Terrible.

Table of Content

Why was the snowman
looking through the carrots?

He was picking his nose!

What do you get if you cross
a snowman with a vampire?

Frostbite!

Why did Santa go to music school?

To improve his wrapping skills!

How does a snowman lose weight?

**He waits for the
weather to get warmer.**

What do reindeer say
before they tell a joke?

This one's gonna sleigh you!

What do you call a cat
on the beach at Christmas?

Sandy Claws!

Why don't crabs
celebrate Christmas?

Because they're shellfish!

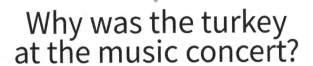

Why was the turkey
at the music concert?

**Because he brought
the drumsticks!**

What do you call a kid
who doesn't believe in Santa?

A rebel without a Claus!

What's Santa's
favorite type of music?

Wrap music!

How do sheep
say Merry Christmas?

Fleece Navidad!

Why did Frosty
go to the Christmas party?

He thought it would be cool.

3

What kind of motorbike
does Santa ride?

A "Holly" Davidson!

Why did no one bid for
Rudolph and Blitzen on eBay?

Because they were two deer!

How does Santa keep track
of all the fireplaces he's visited?

He keeps a log!

Why do mummies
like Christmas so much?

They enjoy all the wrapping!

What do you call a snowman
with a six-pack?

An abdominal snowman.

Why was the Christmas tree
so bad at knitting?

It kept dropping its needles!

What do you call an elf that sings?

A wrapper!

Why does Santa
have three gardens?

So he can "ho ho ho"!

What do elves
post on social media?

Elfies!

What did one Christmas tree
say to the other?

Lighten up!

Why did Santa's helper
see a therapist?

He had low "elf"-esteem!

Why don't you ever see Santa
in a hospital?

Because he has private elf care!

What do you get if you eat Christmas decorations?

Tinsilitis!

What's the difference between the Christmas alphabet and the regular alphabet?

alphabet has no "L"!

What do you get when you cross a bell with a skunk?

Jingle smells!

Why does everyone love Frosty the Snowman?

He's snow joke!

Why did the gingerbread man
go to the doctor?

He was feeling crummy.

What do you call Santa
when he takes a break?

Santa Pause.

What's Santa's favorite candy?

Jolly Ranchers!

What do you call a greedy elf?

Elfish!

What do snowmen
eat for breakfast?

Frosted flakes!

How does Santa get
his Christmas tree home?

He uses a sleigh to get the fir.

Why don't you ever
fight with a reindeer?

They'll always butt heads!

What do you get if you cross
Santa with a detective?

Santa Clues!

Why is Christmas so great
for everyone?

It's a Claus for celebration!

How does a snowman
get around?

By riding an "icicle"!

What's a snowman's
favorite drink?

Iced tea!

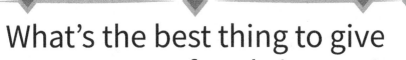

What's the best thing to give
your parents for Christmas?

A list of everything you want!

What do Santa's elves
use to take photos?

Elf-ies!

Why did Santa go to the bakery?

He kneaded some dough!

What's Santa's favorite snack?

Crisp Pringles!

How does a penguin
build its house?

Igloos it together!

What did the beaver
say to the Christmas tree?

Nice gnawing you!

Why was the Christmas tree
so good at sewing?

It was made of needles!

Why did the Christmas tree
break up with the ornaments?

It couldn't handle the hang-ups!

What do you get if you
cross a bell with a skunk?

Jingle smells!

What do snowmen
eat for dessert?

Ice crispies!

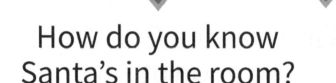

How do you know
Santa's in the room?

You can sense his presents!

Why is everyone thirsty
at the North Pole?

No well.

What did Santa say
when his sleigh broke down?

Oh deer!

Why did the ornaments
go to therapy?

They were feeling so hung up!

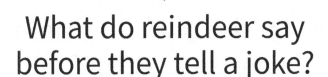

What do reindeer say
before they tell a joke?

This one will sleigh you!

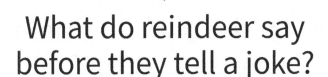

What does Santa suffer from
if he gets stuck in a chimney?

Claus-trophobia!

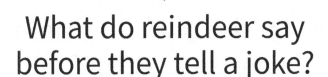

What do you call
Frosty the Snowman's dog?

A slush puppy!

Why don't Christmas trees
ever go to school?

**They already have
too many roots!**

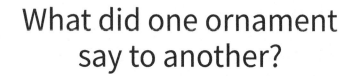

What did one ornament
say to another?

I like hanging with you!

What do you call
a reindeer ghost?

Cari-boo!

Why did the skeleton
refuse to go caroling?

He had no body to go with!

How do Christmas trees
keep themselves safe?

They wear pine-ting!

Why did the turkey
sit on the Christmas lights?

He wanted to lighten up!

What's every parent's
favorite Christmas carol?

Silent Night!

Why did no one bid for
Rudolph and Blitzen on eBay?

Because they were two deer!

What's Santa's favorite thing
to do in the garden?

Hoe, hoe, hoe!

Why did the gingerbread man
start a band?

He had good drum sticks!

Why was the candy cane
so polite?

It was raised in mint condition!

What did the Christmas lights
say to the other lights?

You're lit!

Why does Santa use GPS?

**Because he doesn't want
to be a lost Claus!**

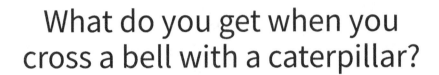

What do you get when you
cross a bell with a caterpillar?

A jingle bug!

Why did the snowman
bring a broom?

**He wanted to
sweep up the competition!**

What did one reindeer say
say to the other?

I sleigh all day!

Why don't Christmas trees sew?

They're afraid of needles!

Where do Santa's reindeer
stop for coffee?

Star-bucks!

What's a snowman's
favorite cereal?

Frosted Flakes!

What's Santa's favorite
type of sandwich?

A jingle ham!

Why was the snowman so brave?

He had a heart of cold!

What did Santa say
to the misbehaving elf?

You're on thin ice!

How does a snowman
lose weight?

He waits until it warms up!

Why don't reindeer tell secrets?

**Because they'll "sleigh"
you with them!**

Knock, knock.   Who's there?

Holly.   Holly who?

Holly-days are here again!

Knock, knock.   Who's there?

Noah.   Noah who?

Noah good Christmas joke?

Knock, knock.   Who's there?

Elf.   Elf who?

**Elf you can't guess,
I'm not telling!**

Knock, knock.   Who's there?

Snow.   Snow who?

**Snow way
I'm missing Christmas!**

Knock, knock. Who's there?

Rudolph. Rudolph who?

Rudolph the red-nosed reindeer, of course!

Knock, knock. Who's there?

Yule. Yule who?

Yule be sorry if you miss Christmas!

Knock, knock. Who's there?

Mary . Mary who?

Mary Christmas and a Happy New Year!

Knock, knock. Who's there?

Candy. Candy who?

Candy cane I join the Christmas party?

Knock, knock.   Who's there?
Wreath.   Wreath who?

Wreath a Merry Christmas!

Knock, knock.   Who's there?
Frost.   Frost who?

Frosty the Snowman, duh!

Knock, knock.   Who's there?
Tinsel.   Tinsel who?

**Tinsel all you need
for Christmas cheer!**

Knock, knock.   Who's there?
Merry.   Merry who?

Merry Christmas to you!

Knock, knock.   Who's there?
Blitzen.   Blitzen who?

Blitzen to the Christmas carols!

Knock, knock.   Who's there?
Icicle.   Icicle who?

Icicle all the way to Christmas!

Knock, knock.   Who's there?
Angel.   Angel who?

Angel we have heard on high!

Knock, knock.   Who's there?
Joy.   Joy who?

**Joy to the world,
Christmas is here!**

Knock, knock.   Who's there?
Bell.   Bell who?

**Bell me out,
it's Christmas time!**

Knock, knock.   Who's there?
Ginger.   Ginger who?

Gingerbread is in the oven!

Knock, knock.   Who's there?
Jolly.   Jolly who?

Jolly Christmas to you!

Knock, knock.   Who's there?
Olive.   Olive who?

**Olive the other reindeer
, remember?**

Knock, knock.   Who's there?
Mistle.   Mistle who?

Mistletoe. Want a kiss?

Knock, knock.   Who's there?
Rudy.   Rudy who?

**Rudy can't you guess
it's Christmas?**

Knock, knock.   Who's there?
St. Nick.   St. Nick who?

St. Nick-er than a Christmas tree!

Knock, knock.   Who's there?
Jingle.   Jingle who?

Jingle all the way!

Knock, knock.   Who's there?

Rein.   Rein who?

Reindeer games are the best!

Knock, knock.   Who's there?

Chris.   Chris who?

Chris-mas is coming soon!

Knock, knock.   Who's there?

Claus.   Claus who?

Claus we love Christmas!

Knock, knock.   Who's there?

Tree.   Tree who?

Tree-mendous holiday wishes to you!

27

Knock, knock.   Who's there?

Deck.   Deck who?

**Deck the halls
with boughs of holly!**

Knock, knock.   Who's there?

Snowflake.   Snowflake who?

**Snowflake's the
best way to celebrate!**

Knock, knock.   Who's there?

Stocking.   Stocking who?

Stocking up on holiday treats!

Knock, knock.   Who's there?

Star.   Star who?

Star of wonder, star of light!

Knock, knock.   Who's there?

Carol.   Carol who?

**Carol-oling around
the Christmas tree!**

Knock, knock.   Who's there?

Gloves.   Gloves who?

**Gloves you could
join us for Christmas!**

Knock, knock.   Who's there?

Egg.   Egg who?

Egg-nog, anyone?

Knock, knock.   Who's there?

Santa.   Santa who?

Santa you a Christmas card!

Knock, knock. Who's there?
December. December who?

December to remember!

Knock, knock. Who's there?
Stocking. Stocking who?

**Stocking stuffer,
open your gifts!**

Knock, knock. Who's there?
Cocoa. Cocoa who?

Cocoa and warm by the fire!

Knock, knock. Who's there?
Wrap. Wrap who?

Wrap up, it's cold outside!

Why did the math book look sad?

**Because it had
too many problems.**

Why don't scientists trust atoms?

**Because they
make up everything!**

What's a teacher's favorite nation?

Expla-nation.

Why was the geometry teacher
always tired?

**Because she ran around
in circles.**

Why did the kid
bring a ladder to school?

**Because he wanted to
go to high school!**

Why is history like a fruitcake?

It's full of dates.

What did the student say when
the pencil broke during a test?

"This is pointless!"

Why was the music teacher
so good at math?

**Because they had
perfect pitch.**

Why was the math teacher
such a good singer?

**Because she knew
how to count on her voice.**

Why did the teacher
wear sunglasses to class?

**Because her students
were so bright!**

What do you get when you
cross a teacher with a vampire?

Lots of blood tests.

Why did the computer
go to school?

To improve its byte size!

Why did the science teacher
break up with the biology teacher?

There was no chemistry.

Why don't history teachers
ever tell jokes?

Because they're already ancient.

Why did the student bring
a fishing rod to school?

**Because he wanted to
catch up on his homework!**

What's a math teacher's
favorite dessert?

Pi.

Why do English teachers
love words so much?

**Because they're always
thesaurus hunting.**

Why don't you do
math in the jungle?

**Because if you add 4 and 4,
you get ate!**

Why was the biology book
so popular?

Because it had all the cells.

What's a teacher's favorite thing
about the beach?

The school of fish.

What did the buffalo say to
his son when he left for school?

Bison.

Why was the broom
late for school?

It swept in.

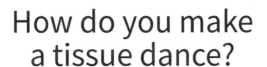

How do you make
a tissue dance?

Put a little boogie in it!

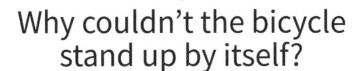

Why couldn't the bicycle
stand up by itself?

It was two-tired.

What do you call a sleeping bull?

A bulldozer.

Why do books alway
get cold in class?

Because they start with a draft!

Why don't skeletons
fight in school?

They don't have the guts.

Why did the teacher
jump into the pool?

To test the water!

What did one pencil say to the other
on the first day of school?

"You're looking sharp!"

What's the hardest subject
for a ghost?

Boo-ology.

Why did the kid study
in the airplane?

**He wanted to get
a higher education.**

Why can't you trust
an algebra teacher?

**They're always
plotting something.**

Why did the clock
go to detention?

**Because it kept ticking
everyone off!**

Why was the history book
always tired?

**Because it had
too many chapters.**

What did the pirate say
on the first day of school?

"Arrr you ready to learn?"

Why did the math student
refuse to play hide-and-seek?

**Because good students
never count out their problems.**

How does the moon
cut his hair?

Eclipse it.

Why did the algebra teacher
miss class?

She sprained her X.

What kind of school do you go
if you're an ice cream cone?

Sundae school.

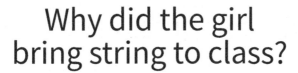

Why did the girl
bring string to class?

**Because she wanted to
tie up loose ends!**

Why don't dads play
hide and seek with their kids?

**Because good luck
hiding the dad bod!**

Why did the dad bring
a ladder to the bar?

**Because he heard the drinks
were on the house.**

What do you call a fake noodle?

An impasta!

My dad's computer caught a cold.

He must have left a window open.

My dad quit his job
as an archeologist.

Now his career is in ruins.

I used to be addicted
to the hokey pokey

but I turned myself around.

Did you hear about the father
who cut off his left leg?

He's all right now.

I never liked my dad's facial hair

**But now it's starting to
grow on me.**

42

What do you call your dad
when he falls through the ice?

A popsicle!

My dad bought a pair of
camouflage pants.

Now I can't find him.

My dad used to say,
Do you think money grows on trees?

And then he got into Bitcoin...

My father doesn't like trees.

He thinks they're shady.

Why did the scarecrow
become a dad?

**Because he was
outstanding in his field.**

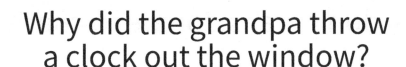

Why did the grandpa throw
a clock out the window?

He wanted to see time fly.

My wife told me I should
do lunges to stay in shape.

That would be a big step forward.

I got my dad a book
about glue once.

He couldn't put it down.

My dad won't play
cards in the jungle.

**He says there are
too many cheetahs.**

Why don't crabs donate to charity?

Because they're shellfish.

My dad wanted to listen to music
while we were fishing.

So I put on something catchy.

What's orange and sounds
like a parrot?

A carrot.

What did the papa cow
say to the baby cow?

It's pasture bedtime.

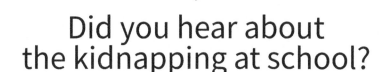

Did you hear about
the kidnapping at school?

It's fine, he woke up!

My dad really loves math.

And then sum.

Why did the bicycle fall over?

Because it was two tired!

What do lobsters do
on Father's Day?

Shellabrate their dads.

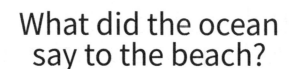

What did the ocean
say to the beach?

Nothing, it just waved.

Where do cows go on dates?

The moo-vies.

I'm reading a book on anti-gravity.

It's impossible to put down!

What has four wheels and flies?

A garbage truck.

Why can't you hear a pterodactyl go to the bathroom?

Because the 'P' is silent!

When is a door not a door?

When it's ajar.

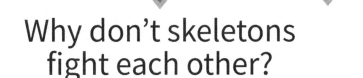

Why don't skeletons fight each other?

They don't have the guts.

What do you call a moose
with no name?

Anonymoose.

How do you make
a tissue dance?

Put a little boogie in it.

Where do cows get their clothes?

From cattle-logs.

When my daughter said
she wanted a pony,

**I said,
Honey, I don't have stable income.**

My father used to be
afraid of hurdles.

But he got over it.

How do Eskimos
fix broken dishes?

With igloo.

Why did the belt
go to jail?

It held up a pair of pants.

What do you call a rude cow?

Beef jerky.

Why did the turkey
refuse dessert?

It was already stuffed!

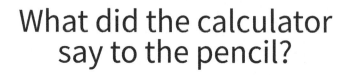

What did the calculator
say to the pencil?

You can count on me!

Why don't mummies
take vacations?

**They're afraid
they'll relax and unwind.**

What is a New Year's resolution?

**Something that goes in
one year and out the other.**

Why did the Easter egg hide?

It was a little chicken.

Why don't you iron
four-leaf clovers?

**You don't want to
press your luck.**

Why did the firecracker
break up with the sparkler?

**It found someone
more explosive.**

What did the pumpkin
say to the pie?

You've got filling to do!

What do you call
two birds in love?

Tweet-hearts.

Why don't ghosts like
to go out in the rain?

It dampens their spirits.

Why did the man dump his
girlfriend at the clock factory?

**She was just
too time-consuming.**

What do you get when you cross
the Easter Bunny with an onion?

A bunion!

Why did the leprechaun
go outside?

To sit on his "paddy" o'.

What's a firecracker's
favorite candy?

Pop rocks!

What key won't open any doors?

A turkey.

What did the stamp say to
the envelope on Valentine's Day?

I'm stuck on you!

What do you call
a witch's garage?

A broom closet.

Where can you practice math
on New Year's Eve?

Times Square.

How do you make Easter easier?

Replace the "t" with an "i."

Why did the Irish potato
turn down a date?

He wasn't peeling it.

What did the flag
say to the pole?

Nothing, it just waved.

Why did the cranberry
turn red?

**Because it saw
the turkey dressing!**

What do you call
a very small Valentine?

A Valen-tiny.

Why don't vampires
have many friends?

**Because they are a pain
in the neck.**

What do you say when someone
asks about your plans for midnight?

"I'll be watching the ball drop!"

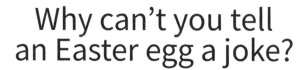

Why can't you tell
an Easter egg a joke?

It might crack up.

What happens if you cross
poison ivy with a four-leaf clover?

You get a rash of good luck.

Why was the American flag
so good at school?

It had lots of stars!

What's the most musical
part of the turkey?

The drumsticks.

What do you call
a ghost's true love?

His ghoul-friend.

How do you make
a skeleton laugh?

Tickle its funny bone.

What's a cow's favorite way
to ring in the New Year?

With a "moo"-sical celebration.

What's the Easter Bunny's
favorite sport?

Basket-ball.

What did the shamrock say
to the leprechaun?

You're "clover"-rated!

What do you call a duck
on July 4th?

A fire-quacker!

What did the turkey say
to the computer?

Google, google, google!

Why shouldn't you fall in love
with a pastry chef?

They'll just dessert you.

What do you call two witches
living together?

Broom-mates.

What do you call always having
a date for New Year's Eve?

Social security!

Why don't rabbits
ever get hot?

They have hare conditioning.

I tried to take up yoga,

**but I'm not flexible enough
to fit it into my schedule.**

I would do crunches,

**but that sounds like it could
interfere with my snack time.**

What's a vegetable's
favorite form of self-care?

Meditating-it.

I started running,

**but I keep finding myself
back at the fridge.**

Why did the tomato
go to therapy?

**It had too many layers
of emotional baggage.**

I bought a juicer,

**but all it's done is juice up
my credit card bill.**

I thought about going on
a juice cleanse,

**but I decided I needed
a pizza cleanse first.**

What did the almond say
to the peanut at the gym?

**I'm 'nut' working out
without you!**

How does the broccoli
keep in shape?

It does cauliflower-etics.

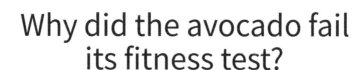

Why did the avocado fail
its fitness test?

**It couldn't make it
past the dips.**

Why don't skeletons
work out?

They don't have the guts for it!

I tried to exercise,
but the weights didn't lift themselves,

so I gave up.

What do you call
a fake noodle at the gym?

An impasta.

My diet always starts tomorrow.
Today's just a cheat day...

**and yesterday...
and the day before that.**

I don't trust people
who run marathons.

**They seem to be running
away from something.**

Why did the gym close down?

It just didn't work out.

I'm on a 30-day diet.
So far,

I've lost 15 days.

I was going to eat a salad,
but then I thought,

'What would my pizza think?'

I told my trainer I want abs.

**He told me to try
laughing more.**

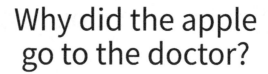

Why did the apple
go to the doctor?

It wasn't peeling well.

Exercise?

I thought you said extra fries!

I started a fitness class,

but I think they were lying about it being fun.

What did the runner eat before their marathon?

Nothing—they fasted!

I'm into fitness...

Fitness whole pizza in my mouth!

66

Why did the banana
go to the gym?

It wanted to peel better.

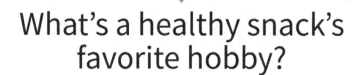

What's a healthy snack's
favorite hobby?

**Going on
a fruit-ful adventure.**

Why do avocados
never go to the gym?

**They're already
the good kind of fat.**

I thought about going vegan,

**but I love cheese more than
I love feeling good about myself.**

What do you call someone
who's trying to get into shape?

A 'work-in-progress.'

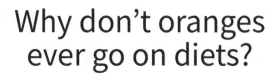

Why don't oranges
ever go on diets?

**They don't want to get
squeezed out of the fun.**

Why did the grape
go to the doctor?

It was feeling winey.

Why did the lettuce
break up with the tomato?

It just wasn't romaine-ing loyal.

I bought a bike to get healthy.

**Now I just need to remember
where I parked it.**

My New Year's resolution
is to exercise more.

**I'm already tired
just thinking about it.**

How do vegetables
travel to the gym?

By car-rot.

Why did the zucchini
bring weights to the kitchen?

**It was trying
to squash the competition.**

I tried to get on a healthy diet,

**but food keeps talking behind my back.
Especially cake!**

Why did the kale
go to therapy?

**It had too
many greens of anxiety.**

What's the healthiest way
to eat your emotions?

**With a side of veggies,
of course!**

Why don't we ever tell secrets
at the salad bar?

**Because the dressing
is always listening!**

Why don't eggs tell jokes?

They'd crack each other up.

What's a taco's favorite music?

Wrap music.

What did the sushi
say to the bee?

Wasabi!

Why don't oranges ever go out?

**They're just too juicy
for drama.**

Why did the tomato turn red?

**Because it saw
the salad dressing.**

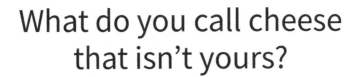

What do you call cheese
that isn't yours?

Nacho cheese!

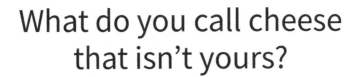

Why did the bread
go to therapy?

It had too many crumby issues.

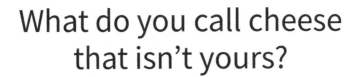

Why don't bananas
ever get lonely?

**Because they hang out
in bunches.**

Why did the coffee
file a police report?

It got mugged.

What do you call
fake spaghetti?

An impasta.

Why did the cookie
go to the doctor?

It was feeling crumby.

Why did the pepper
break up with the salt?

**Because it was
too spicy to settle down.**

Why did the grape stop
in the middle of the road?

It ran out of juice.

Why do mushrooms
make great friends?

**Because they're such fungi
to be around.**

What did one slice of bread
to the other at the party?

Let's loaf together!

Why was the cucumber
so mad?

Because it was in a pickle.

74

What do you call
a sad strawberry?

A blueberry.

What did the apple
say to the orange?

Nothing, apples don't talk.

What's the best way
to enjoy a hot dog?

Relish it.

How do you make
an artichoke laugh?

You tickle its heart.

Why was the
baby tomato crying?

**Because it couldn't
ketchup to its parents.**

Why did the banana
go to school?

To learn how to peel.

Why can't you trust tacos?

They always spill the beans.

Why did the carrot
get invited to the party?

**Because it was a rootin
' tootin' good time!**

What do you call
a snowman's breakfast?

Frosted flakes.

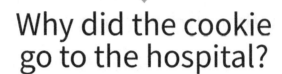

Why did the cookie
go to the hospital?

It felt crummy.

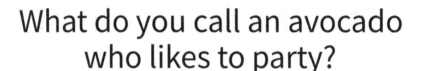

What do you call an avocado
who likes to party?

A guac-star.

Why don't burgers
ever tell secrets?

**Because they might
spill the beans.**

77

What's a pretzel's
favorite dance?

The twist.

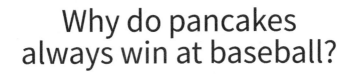

Why do pancakes
always win at baseball?

They have the batter.

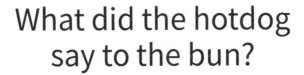

What did the hotdog
say to the bun?

**Stop loafing around
and ketchup!**

What's a potato's
favorite game?

Mashed tag.

Why don't melons get married?

Because they cantaloupe.

What's a chef's
favorite horror movie?

The Silence of the Yams.

Why was
the peanut butter upset?

**Because it felt
spread too thin.**

What do you call a chicken
who tells jokes?

A comedi-hen.

Why do fish neve
do well in school?

**Because they're always swinmming
around in their thoughts.**

What's orange
and sounds like a parrot?

A carrot.

Why did the lettuce
win the race?

**Because it was
ahead of the pack!**

How do you fix
a broken pizza?

With tomato paste.

Why don't cats
play poker in the wild?

Too many cheetahs.

What do you call
a dog magician?

A labracadabrador.

Why don't fish
play basketball?

**They're
afraid of the net.**

Why did the cow
go to space?

To see the moooon.

81

Why are fish so smart?

Because they live in schools.

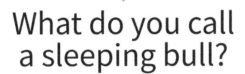

What do you call
a sleeping bull?

A bulldozer.

Why did the elephant
bring a suitcase to the zoo?

**Because it was going on
a trunk-cation.**

Why don't oysters
share their pearls?

Because they're shellfish.

What do you call a cold dog?

A chili dog.

Why do bees have sticky hair?

Because they use honeycombs.

Why are frogs
always so happy?

**Because they eat
whatever bugs them.**

What do you call
an alligator in a vest?

An investi-gator.

Why did the chicken
join the band?

Because it had the drumsticks.

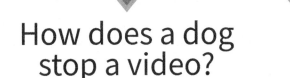

How does a dog
stop a video?

By hitting the paws button.

What do you call
a group of singing cats?

A meow-sical.

Why did the duck get a job?

To make some bills.

Why are cats bad storytellers?

Because they only have one tail.

Why did the crab never share?

Because he was shellfish.

What do you call a bear
with no teeth?

A gummy bear.

Why did the turtle
cross the road?

To get to the shell station.

What do you call an animal
you keep in your car?

A carpet.

Why do cows wear bells?

Because their horns don't work.

What did the cat say
when it saw a bowl of food?

"You've got to be kitten me!"

Why did the snake
lose the debate?

It had no legs to stand on.

What's a dog's favorite
homework assignment?

A chew-sday.

What do you call a parrot
who won't stop talking?

A polly-gab.

Why don't seagulls
fly over the bay?

Because then they'd be bagels.

Why did the farmer
ride his horse into town?

**Because it was
too heavy to carry.**

What do you call
a cow that can't moo?

A milk dud.

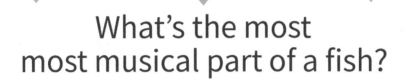

What's the most
most musical part of a fish?

The scales.

What do you get when you
cross a sheep and a kangaroo?

A woolly jumper.

Why don't dogs dance?

Because they have two left feet.

How does a penguin
build its house?

Igloos it together.

Why did the dog
sit in the shade?

**Because it didn't
want to be a hot dog.**

What do you call
a pig that knows karate?

A pork chop.

Why do giraffes
have such long necks?

Because their feet stink.

What do you get when you
cross a crocodile with a GPS?

A navigator.

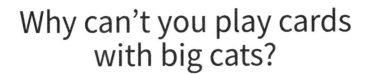

Why can't you play cards
with big cats?

Because they're all cheetahs.

What do you call
a frog that parks illegally?

Toad.

Why are elephants
always ready for vacation?

They have trunks packed!

Why did the football coach
go to the bank?

To get his quarterback.

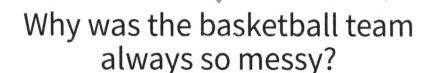

Why was the basketball team
always so messy?

**They couldn't make
any clean shots!**

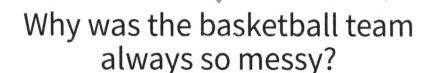

Why don't basketball players
ever go on vacation?

**Because they'd get called
for traveling.**

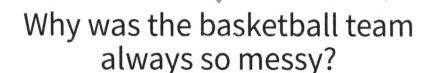

Why did the golfer
bring two pairs of pants?

In case he got a hole-in-one.

Why do soccer players
do well in school?

**They know how to use
their heads.**

Why don't tennis players
get married?

**Because love means
nothing to them.**

Why is it always so hot
at baseball games?

Because all the fans left.

Why did the baseball team
go to the bakery?

To get their batter.

Why couldn't the bicycle
stand up by itself?

It was two-tired.

Why was the football team
always so good at music?

**they were good with the
"kickoffs."**

Why did the soccer player
bring string to the game?

To tie the score.

Why did the golfer
need new socks?

Because he had a hole-in-one.

Why did the referee
go to school?

**He wanted to improve
his whistle-blowing skills.**

Why can't you play
sports in the jungle?

**Because there are
too many cheetahs.**

Why don't skeletons
play basketball?

They don't have the guts.

Why did the baseball player
get arrested?

Because he stole second base.

Why are frogs
so good at basketball?

**Because they always
make jump shots.**

Why did the golfer bring
an extra club?

He wanted to "swing" by.

Why was Cinderella
so bad at soccer?

**She kept running away
from the ball.**

Why are swimmers so
so smart?

They always go with the flow.

95

What's a cheerleader's
favorite color?

Yell-o!

Why did the volleyball team
sleep in?

They couldn't get set.

Why don't boxers
have many friends?

**Because they're always trying
to punch above their weight.**

Why did the baseball player
bring a pencil?

In case he had to draw a walk.

What's a gymnast's
favorite food?

A balance snack.

Why did the football player
go to art school?

**He wanted to
learn how to draw plays.**

Why don't race car drivers
ever get lost?

**Because they always take
the fastest route.**

Why are hockey players
great comedians?

**They always get
good ice-breakers.**

Why don't athletes
like to go bowling?

**Because they get tired
of striking out.**

Why do marathon runners
never get lost?

They always follow the course.

Why don't baseball players
ever tell secrets?

**Because they always
throw curveballs.**

What do you call a pig
that plays basketball?

A ball hog.

Why did the tennis player
bring a ladder?

To serve higher.

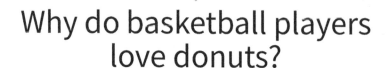

Why do basketball players
love donuts?

They can dunk them!

Why do football players
love party games?

**Because they always
bring a good defense.**

Why was the soccer player
a great singer?

She had perfect pitch!

What do you call a person who can't stop watching football?

A goal-oriented individual.

Why are baseball players always bad bowlers?

Because they can't stop leaving splits.

What's a golfer's worst nightmare?

The sandman because he's always stuck in the bunker.

Why did the basketball player bring a flashlight?

Because he was afraid of getting dunked in the dark!

Made in the USA
Monee, IL
21 November 2024

70845669R00059